"Getting there
is half the fun!"

...but not if you're
on a diet...

To my thin friends,
Miriam Polster, Iris Goodman,
and Gloria Penner-Snyder,
who for the 20 years I have known them
have never worried about that extra pound.

My gratitude to the companion of my dreams,
Herman Gadon, who loves me as I am, and my
appreciation to my live-in secretary and cook,
Pamela Morgan, who edits my writings and my
meals, and my heartfelt thanks to my wonderful editor,
Patti Wayant, with whom I've shared moments of great
introspection as well as moments of great hilarity.

If I Eat I Feel Guilty, If I Don't I'm Deprived

...and Other Dilemmas of Daily Life

Natasha Josefowitz, Ph.D.

Blue Mountain Press™

SPS Studios, Inc., Boulder, Colorado

Library of Congress Catalog Card Number: 00-010652
ISBN: 0-88396-568-2

Certain trademarks are used under license.

Manufactured in the United States of America
First Printing: December 2000

This book is printed on fine quality, laid embossed, 80 lb. paper. This paper has been specifically produced to be acid free (neutral pH) and contains no groundwood or unbleached pulp. It conforms with all the requirements of the American National Standards Institute, Inc. to ensure that this book will last and be enjoyed by future generations.

 This book is printed on recycled paper.

Library of Congress Cataloging-in-Publication Data

Josefowitz, Natasha.
     If I eat I feel guilty, if I don't I'm deprived, and other dilemmas of daily life / Natasha Josefowitz.
          p. cm.
     ISBN 0-88396-568-2
     1. Food habits—Poetry. 2. Eating disorders—Poetry. I. Title.
PS3560.O768 I38 2000
811'.54—dc21

                                                                                              00-010652
                                                                                                    CIP

SPS Studios, Inc.
P.O. Box 4549, Boulder, Colorado 80306

Contents

7 If I Eat I Feel Guilty,
  If I Don't I'm Deprived
8 Diets
8 Will Power
9 Almost...
9 My Life Is Made Up Of...
10 The People Inside Me
11 Hopeless Quest
11 I Was Born in the Wrong Century
12 Thin Tricks
12 Too Many of Us...
13 Quality of Life
14 Tossing and Turning
15 False Expectations
16 Judgment Days
17 Love Chains
18 Meeting New Men
19 I Can't Get Rid of "Me"
20 The Spa Experience
20 Losing Battles
21 There Is a Thing on the Floor
22 The Storeroom
24 Mixed Berries
26 Blissful Moments
26 The Philosopher Said:
27 Making a Difference
28 Mail-Order Shopping
29 Bargains!
29 More
30 Asked to Help Out
31 Can't Do It All!
32 The Box of Chocolates
32 Daily Dilemmas
33 I'm Always Tired

34 She Feels Guilty Because...
36 What Women Want...
37 Cooking with Calories
37 In My Cookbook...
38 Room Service
38 No Time
39 The Gourmet Meal
40 Leftovers
40 Round Robin
41 The Cookie Exchange
42 The Soup Stock
42 Calorie Saver
43 The Celebration
44 The Diet Workshop
46 Unsuccessful Shopping
47 I Should Know Better
47 Curing Fevers and Colds
48 Is It Real?
49 At Work
49 Relearnings
50 Stop the World,
  I Want to Get Off!
52 Exercise
53 Remember Food?
54 The Nutrition Jungle
56 And Yet, I Still Ask
57 Entertaining
58 To Grandmother's House
  for the Holidays
60 Authority Figures?
61 What Do I Really Want?
62 The Grass Is Always Greener
63 Little Pleasures
64 About the Author

If I Eat I Feel Guilty,
If I Don't I'm Deprived

I am an addict
I have a real addiction
It is not alcohol or drugs
It is not smoking
It is food

I love to eat
and even when I'm not hungry
I will eat chocolate chip cookies
or strawberry ice cream

I can gain three pounds
after one good meal
and starve myself
for three weeks
to lose them again

When I'm upset
I eat for comfort
when I'm happy
I eat for joy
when I'm bored
I eat to fill up the time

When I'm tired
I eat to get energy
even when I'm very busy
I eat just in case
I won't have time to later

I am an addict
and live my life
feeling deprived
when I don't indulge
and feeling guilty when I do

Diets

No bread
with strawberry jam
no rich desserts
no candy
no chocolate ice cream
no french fries
no chips

INSTEAD

Carrot sticks
raw cauliflower
with a low-fat yogurt dip
broiled fish
cottage cheese
lettuce with a diet dressing
half a grapefruit
one salt-free cracker

Even if I don't live longer
it certainly will seem longer

Will Power

I have will power
For everything
Except for what's fattening
When it comes to food
I can't resist
I wait five minutes
Trying to talk myself out of it
Then eat it anyway
And even take a second helping
Kicking myself all along
For having no will power
Help!

Almost...

I always set goals
beyond my reach —
getting there is half the fun

I always dream
of wondrous things —
but wishing itself is
fulfilling

So I raise my hopes
even if in vain
and do not discount
the pleasure
of the fantasy
And whatever happens
I am grateful for
the time of "Almost"

My Life Is Made Up Of...

An infinite number
of insignificant details
a large number
of significant ones
and a daily dose
of emergencies

The People Inside Me

There are people inside me —
Some I know well
others are lurking in the shadows
A few I love and am even proud of
A few I'm ashamed of
and sometimes try to discard

The people inside me
often disagree with one another —
When one thinks I should diet
another wants to eat
When one is boastful
another reprimands her for being a braggart

The people inside me
have different aspirations —
One is ambitious and very visible
another wants to lead a quiet life
One takes work with her on ski vacations
another prefers lounging in the sun

So I must live with passion
yet try for moderation —
with self-confidence
yet with doubts —
looking out for myself
yet being there for others

For I am all of the people inside me

Hopeless Quest

Since I was twelve years old
I've been just a few pounds away
from being really beautiful
And even when I lose those pounds
somehow I'm always still
a couple of pounds away
from being the "right" weight

I Was Born in
the Wrong Century

If I lived in the times of
Rembrandt or Rubens or Renoir
when women who had full breasts
large buttocks, big thighs
and dimples and folds
were considered beautiful
I would be much too thin

But I live in the times of
sports bras, exercise videos
and fashion magazines

and so I'm too fat!

Thin Tricks

If I take many small slivers of cake
instead of one large slice,
I am really eating less.
If I keep evening out
the uneven edges of the pie,
I'm not really eating it.
If I eat off your plate,
I'm not eating off mine.
If I finish the children's leftovers,
it doesn't count.
If I don't order a meal,
but taste everyone else's,
I won't gain weight.
So how come
I'm not thin?

Too Many of Us...

Too many of us
are always dieting
trying to fit
the media image
of the "right size"
knowing that it's hopeless
nevertheless still trying

Too many of us
are unhappy with our bodies
instead of celebrating
health and well-being

Too many of us
see food only as temptation
instead of sustenance
and delight

Quality of Life

I jump out of bed
throw on some clothes
gulp down my coffee
put a note on the fridge
wave to my husband
run out of the house
hop into my car
dash into my office
glance at my mail
scan the paper
scribble a note
get rid of a visitor
cancel a luncheon
order a sandwich
eat at my desk, my ear to the phone
make a rapid decision
hurry to a meeting
refuse an invitation
read a summary
draw a quick conclusion
speed out of the office
go to a fast-food place
pick up a pizza
throw something in the oven
grab a bite
ask him about his day
not really listen
flip through a journal
skim through a report
turn on the TV
watch a ten-minute newscast
blow him a kiss
hit the sack

Tossing and Turning

I can't sleep
and wish you would awaken, too
so that we could chat
about nothing in particular

Perhaps we could talk about
the latest news story
or the kids
It doesn't matter
but I need companionship
in the midst of my restless night

I whisper softly
"Are you sleeping?"
You do not answer
and continue to breathe peacefully
I go to the bathroom
and flush the toilet
You do not stir
I noisily get a glass of water
to no avail

I toss and turn
sigh and groan
but you're so fast asleep
that I would have to
shake you to wake you up
But I cannot do the deed —
feeling too guilty to rob you
of what I wish I had —
sleep

So I'm lying here
feeling miserable
to be sleepless alone
but feeling virtuous
that I do not disturb you

False Expectations

A woman marries a man
expecting that he will change
but he doesn't

A man marries a woman
expecting that she won't change
and she does

Judgment Days

When I criticize my children
I see it as sign of caring
They take it as disapproval
and overreact

When a friend criticizes me
I take it as a gift
an opportunity to improve
and I'm grateful

Yet when my mother
criticizes me
I'm insulted

Love Chains

I do not expect
my children
to love me
the way
I love them

However
if they love
their children
that same way
my love
will have come
full circle

Meeting New Men

When I meet a new man,
the more handsome he is
the less attractive I feel;
the more intelligent he is
the stupider I sound;
the smoother he is
the more awkward I seem.

In other words,
when I meet a man
I really like,
I become this blubbering idiot
and he will have nothing to do with me.

When I meet a man
I'm not interested in,
I am beautiful, brilliant,
witty and fun,
so he falls madly in love
with me,
but I will have nothing to do
with him.

The trick is to be dull
with the men I don't like
and sparkling with the ones I do,
but for some reason,
it's always the other way around.

I Can't Get Rid of "Me"

The problem is
that wherever I go
I take "me" along
So every time
I plan to change
or do something
in a different way
there I am again
tagging along
getting in the way
and doing everything
in that same old
dysfunctional
ineffective
irritating
unchanging way

The Spa Experience

Carol says stretch
Jody says bend
Linda says lift
Suzanne says swing
Brenda says breathe
Donna says don't eat

I stand at the back
of the exercise class
hoping no one will notice
that I can't sit
with my legs straight
can't touch my toes
can't straighten my back
can't bend sideways

I lag behind on the morning walk
overtaken by the eighty-year-old lady
and the six-year-old child

I am first only in the dining room

Losing Battles

By trying to be
everywhere at once
I am nowhere

By trying to be
everything to too many
I am no one

There Is a Thing on the Floor

There is a thing on the floor
an object that inspires
dread in me

It has the power to
make me feel guilty
and depressed all day
or proud of my achievements

I wish I could avoid it
but it is there waiting for me
drawing me to it every morning
and sometimes in the evening, too

I step on it ever so gingerly
hoping for good news
Even if I have been steadfast the day before
I never step on it with confidence

This thing on my floor
this object
controls my life
I hate it yet cannot get rid of it

It is my enemy
It is my friend
It is the bathroom scale

The Storeroom

Every January first
we vow to clean up the storeroom
We plan to open all those boxes
that never got unpacked
in twenty years and many moves

Until one day I said to my husband
"Either we move to a bigger house
or we clean out the storeroom"

So we set aside two weekends
rolled up our sleeves
and did the deed

There were boxes on top of boxes
shelves filled with things
we'll never use

scarves and mittens
hardened ski wax
rusted batteries inside of toys

a coffee maker
an ice bucket
paper plates from parties past

out-of-style hats
an old fur blanket
children's books and roller skates

my son's soap sculptures
from kindergarten
my daughter's drawings
from first grade

mountain boots
some empty frames
a jigsaw puzzle with missing pieces

As we sort through
a lifetime of objects
memories tumble out, too

Some make us smile
as we remember
some tug and hurt as we discard

Then everything goes back in boxes
most labeled "For donation"
and stacked again
but in the driveway
not in the storeroom
which now stands empty
of memories

Mixed Berries

Some are blueberries
some are blackberries
some are called strawberries or raspberries
loganberries and huckleberries
but all berries need to be eaten
with cream — milk won't do — and sugar
in a gold-rimmed bowl
with a silver spoon
on a sunlit terrace
in a garden chair
in dappled shade
wearing a large straw hat
with a flowing ribbon
striped with little flowers
and a pale green shawl
draped casually over the shoulders
in case of a cooler breeze
a small white dog
asleep in a corner
a side table with a cup of tea
or perhaps lemonade
or a glass of champagne

with a cookie
or a piece of cake
with candied fruit and raisins in it
a box of chocolates —
the kind with almonds
or maybe hazelnuts —
some field flowers
picked by the children
in a crystal vase
hand-blown in Austria
the intermittent song of a bird
the muffled sound of a piano
maybe Mozart, maybe not
the scent of night-blooming jasmine
or is it orange blossoms?

But now, the tea is getting cold
the champagne, warm
the chocolates are melting in the sun
the birds are waiting
for a crumb to fall
It's time to eat the berries
the blueberries, the blackberries
the raspberries, the strawberries
with cream and sugar
in a gold-rimmed bowl
It's time to eat the berries

Blissful Moments

Eating a ripe peach
bought at the farmer's market
that previous Sunday
and smelling a gardenia
picked from my garden
a few minutes ago
while listening to some unidentified
guitar music on the radio
sitting in my reclining arm chair
writing this to capture
that memory forever

The Philosopher Said:

To be happy
you need freedom
but it takes courage
to be free

I Say:

If we have the courage
to be free
we will have the freedom
to be happy

Making a Difference

helping others
giving to others
being there for others

one hand extended
to touch another
one ear bent over
to hear the unspoken
eyes wide open
to see the unseen

a mouth whispering
a consolation
a heart willing
to soothe the pain
a mind ready
to solve a problem

a person there
a volunteer
an angel
making a difference

helping others
giving to others
being there for others
are also gifts
we give to ourselves

Mail-Order Shopping

The catalogues come in the mail
If I'm too busy
I throw them away
but here and there
I take some
delicious moments
to look through the catalogues
skipping the housewares, the tools
the electronic equipment, the food
and getting to the fashions

There, the tall, slim, hipless models
with not a single hair out of place
smile with perfect teeth
and on every page
look smashing in everything
from bathing suits to cocktail dresses

I try to picture
my shorter, plumper body
in the beckoning clothes
The saleslady on the phone
assures me of prompt delivery

A few days later
the package arrives
The material is not what I expected
the dress is too small or unbecoming
or just never looks the same on me
as on those cheerful models
and if there is one item that fits
it doesn't go with anything I own
and so with hope springing eternal
I look through the catalogues again

Bargains!

I love to buy
but I hate to spend

So I go to discount stores
warehouse clearances
bargain basements
special sales
closeouts

And I come home with things
that end up
in garage sales
charity bazaars
the Salvation Army
and other places
where people go
who love to buy
but hate to spend

More

We are told:
buy more
use more
spend more
do more
travel more
watch more TV
surf the Net
fax more
e-mail
call more
Whatever we do
it is not enough
Whatever we are
we are not good
enough

So, forever made
to be dissatisfied
we comply
by eating more

Asked to Help Out

Asked to help out
  I say yes, of course
Could you pick her up?
  Yes, it's on my way
Would you baby-sit?
  Yes, with pleasure
Give us a hand?
  Yes I'll be glad to
  I'll write it up
  send it in
  fax it
  call
  run the errand
  visit the sick
  bring chicken soup
  mail the card
Do you mind?
May I impose?
Just this time?
  The answer is always
  yes
  What would happen
  if I said no...
  I'm busy
  I'm tired
  I don't feel like it
  I just don't want to?
  The answer is
  NO
  I tried
  and nothing bad
  happened
  so now I say
  NO
  when I don't feel
  like saying YES

Can't Do It All!

If I do this
I won't get that done
If I do that
this will slip by
If I do both
neither will be perfect

Not everything worth doing
is worth doing well

Because there is too much
of everything
There is not enough
of anything

The Box of Chocolates

My favorite kind…
truffles with nuts.
Where can I put them
so that I'm not tempted?
Nowhere.
All day I think of them…
visualizing the neat brown rows,
tasting the indescribable flavor.
If I eat one,
I'll eat two.
No, three, four, the box.
It's easy.
As soon as I'm finished
I will hate myself for hours.
It's either obsession with deprivation
or gluttony with guilt.
Next time
please bring me flowers.

Daily Dilemmas

If I take a soft drink
I get the sugar,
calories, and cavities.

If I choose a diet drink
I get chemicals
and a chance at cancer.

I'm not always sure
whether I'd rather
die young but thin
or old and fat.

I'm Always Tired

Household chores
are never done.
There is always
one more thing
that needs to be cleaned,
cooked, mended,
or put away.

Work is also never done.
There is always
one more item
that needs to be studied,
written, calculated,
or filed away.

I'm always catching up,
but I'm never "caught up."
When I think I have finished,
terminated, accomplished,
resolved everything,
there is always
one more thing
that needs to get done.

She Feels Guilty Because...

She feels guilty because
she is too skinny
or because she gained weight

She feels guilty because
she doesn't call her mother enough
or she's too attached to her

She feels guilty because
she needs time alone
or doesn't have enough time for friends

She feels guilty because
she's not assertive enough
or she's too much so

She feels guilty because
she's too thrifty
or she's spending too much

She feels guilty because
she has a career
or she's just a homemaker

She feels guilty because
she doesn't like to cook
or she overfeeds her family

She feels guilty because
she doesn't spend enough time with her children
or she is overprotective

She feels guilty because
she's earning more than her husband
or she's not earning enough

She feels guilty because
she has too many outside activities
or doesn't volunteer enough

But she feels most guilty
because she should be more
like someone else

What Women Want...

To live a life that is
thought out, thought through,
and carefully considered.

To take care of what's not urgent,
instead of living from crisis to crisis,
responding only to emergencies.

To not have to dress in five minutes,
gulp down food in two,
be rushed on the phone,
scribble curt notes to friends,
and run through the house
always late for the next
unscheduled event.

To have time to notice each day,
to take pleasure in living each hour,
to enjoy every minute
before it has ticked away.

Cooking with Calories

Once in a while
I cook a special meal
for my husband who is thin
I use cream instead of yogurt in the soup
make a cheese sauce for the cauliflower
serve steak and potatoes with real butter
and dip strawberries in melted chocolate
He expects steamed, boiled, or broiled
so he is happily surprised
and I delight in cooking for him
unexpected dishes
made with love

In My Cookbook...

The best meals
are the ones
I don't have to cook
What I do best
is make reservations!

Room Service

Hello!
Room Service, please!
I wish to order breakfast:

Two poached eggs
one underdone
the other hard boiled
with one strip of limp bacon
burnt toast
lukewarm coffee
with soured milk
canned orange juice
slightly fermented
half spilled on the tray
and make me wait about an hour please

…This is an unusual order —
    not sure we can fill it!

…Of course you can.
    You did yesterday!

No Time

No time to market
too busy to cook
too tired to go out for dinner

Frozen pizza again tonight!

The Gourmet Meal

She made a wonderful dinner
using all kinds of ingredients
different spices
and complicated sauces

She served it
on china plates
with polished silverware
I was very impressed

When I asked for the recipe
she led me to her kitchen
took down three jars from a shelf
and said, "Just mix this in a pan
and cook for a few minutes"

I was even more impressed

Leftovers

I love
Thanksgiving dinner
with all the trimmings
and eating too much
all afternoon

But best of all
I love the leftovers

Round Robin

When I'm really thin
I feel tired.
When I get tired
I eat.
When I eat
I get fat.
When I'm fat
I get depressed.
When I'm depressed
I eat more.

Wait a minute!
How do I get back
to the first line
when I'm really thin...?

The Cookie Exchange

"Please bring three-dozen cookies
and your recipe,"
said the invitation.
Oh, horrors!
How can I admit
I never baked a cookie
in my life?
I call a friend
who has a daughter
who has a recipe
that is really easy —
and so I do it.
They turn out
big, thick, and gloppy.
Everyone else's
are petits fours — small and dainty.
I am ashamed
until the kids come in
and say,
"Oh, goody,
real cookies!"
And eat mine up first.

The Soup Stock

I cooked some broccoli for dinner
then added its stems and leaves
picked herbs from our garden
boiled it down
to a lovely green stock
and left it to cool
on the kitchen counter
for some future wondrous soup

He saw the jar
with greenish water
and threw it out

Men!

Calorie Saver

I'm so glad the cake was tasteless
that the filling was like glue
that the icing looked like toothpaste
I'm so glad

I'm relieved the dessert was awful
that the ice cream was too soft
that the cookies were like cardboard
I'm relieved

I didn't eat it

The Celebration

I finally made it
I lost ten pounds
I look terrific
My clothes fit well
even a little too loosely

I have new cheekbones
a smaller waist
can tuck in my shirt
instead of trying to hide
my formerly big hips

How shall I celebrate?

With a double scoop of ice cream?
A large slice of New York cheesecake?
A big piece of lemon-meringue pie?
A huge portion of chocolate mousse?
A whole box of candy?

Oh, well!
I guess I'll have some low-fat cottage cheese
on a small salt-free cracker!

The Diet Workshop

We stand in line
anxious
exchanging few words
The moment of truth
is approaching

Will our week of strict observance
pay off
or will we be shamed
into trying harder?

We step on the scale
"You lost a pound!"
The woman in charge is always supportive

We sit and talk
share the triumph
of having resisted a cookie
or not having succumbed
to a second slice of pizza

We give each other tricks, like
don't have sweets in the house
put on your plate only
what you're allowed
eat sitting down
eat slowly
wait ten minutes before
getting another helping
drink lots of water
when you're hungry
do an activity instead
and plan your whole day's meals

And so we learn from one another
how to be slim
and stay that way forever
and in the process
we learn about each other's lives

Every week for an hour
we share the intimacy
of women sitting together
talking about ourselves
talking about our lives

Unsuccessful Shopping

There was no garage
at the garage sale
and no yard was sold
at the yard sale

Didn't see a farmer
at the farmer's market
nor were there any elephants
at the white elephant sale

Saw nothing liquid
at the liquidation sale
nor fire
at the fire sale

No one would swap with me
at the swap meet
and I found no fleas
at the flea market
but perhaps brought some home
after having been there

I Should Know Better

Why do I eat the wrong foods
when I know better —
like sneaking chocolates
in between meals
and regretting it two minutes later?

Why do I order dessert
when I know better —
by saying I'll just have one bite
then eating the whole thing
and regretting it two minutes later?

While some might be able to
exercise consistent control
I always seem to opt for
instant gratification.

Curing Fevers and Colds

Is it that
you starve a fever
and feed a cold?

Or is it the other
way around?

Considering this dilemma
I think I'll just
feed both!

Is It Real?

I was wearing some jewelry
the other day
when someone asked
whether it was real

If it were fake
it would be a compliment
but if it were real
I would be offended

I did not tell

At Work

Men think
they're doing
well
unless criticized

Women think
they're not
doing well
unless praised

Relearnings

Alas...
I often need
to learn again
what I already know!

Stop the World,
I Want to Get Off!

I want to leave the papers
piled so high on my desk
that I cannot find the top of it
I want to leave the dishes
so stacked up in my sink
that I cannot see the bottom of it
I want to leave my clothes-filled hamper
and the empty refrigerator

I want to leave my messy closet
the unswept leaves
in front of the house
the buttons that need
to be sewn on
the hems that need
to be shortened

I want to leave the unmade bed
the dusty shelves
the unpressed shirts
the unanswered calls
the unpaid bills
the unmopped floors
the unwashed windows
the TV that needs
to be fixed

Stop the world
I want to get off
at some other place
at some other time
where I can sit
without feeling guilty
about doing nothing
for an entire afternoon

Exercise

Any excuse not to do it
A slight morning backache
is a welcome impediment
The usual one is
"No time now, I'm late already"
Although I feel better all day
if I exercise in the morning
I manage not to
and luxuriate in bed
feeling deliciously guilty
for another fifteen minutes —
really believing that
"I'll start tomorrow for sure"

Remember Food?

We used to "eat in"
but now we "take out"
It was "home cooked"
now it's "store bought"
We had "hamburger"
now it's "tofu burger"
We used to put "ketchup" on it
now it's "salsa"
We never "deep fry" anything anymore
now we "stir fry" it
We have exchanged old-fashioned ice cream
for low-fat frozen yogurt
Mom's pound cake
comes in a new nonfat version
and our former large mug of coffee
now has to fit into a small cappuccino cup

I remember when food was "delicious"
Now it has to be "healthy"

The Nutrition Jungle

Jogging is good for you
but it's bad for your knees

Eat red meat
the best source of iron
Don't eat red meat —
cholesterol

Eat spinach —
it has folic acid
No don't
it leaches out calcium

Eat calcium
but with vitamin D
which won't get absorbed
without magnesium
which in turn needs zinc
or is it the other way around?

A glass of wine will reduce your LDL level
but may give you breast cancer
Eat more wheat, or is it oats?

Some foods won't let others
be absorbed by the intestinal tract
Some foods need to be eaten in combination

So use less oil
except olive oil
which is rich in omega-3
but avoid palm oil and coconut oil
Saturated is bad
unsaturated is better
hydrogenated is worse

Read the labels
but what do they mean?
Are they additives or preservatives
or artificial colors?
Are they nutritive or toxic?
Will research rats die if they eat it?
Will I?

And Yet, I Still Ask

Is the fish fresh?
Has the corn just been picked?
Did the tomatoes ripen on the vine?
Is the lettuce organic?
Does the soup have MSG?
Is the baking done on the premises?
Is this really fat free?

Questions we ask in
restaurants, farmer's markets
bakeries, and ice cream parlors

No one has ever answered
that the meat is unfit
for human consumption
that the vegetables are full of pesticides
and the fruit was picked green
several weeks ago

No one has ever said that
the cake is mostly preservatives
the peaches will rot
before they will ripen
and the food has been sitting
on the counter for hours

And yet, I still ask...

Entertaining

When my mother entertained
she used her best china
crystal, and silverware
and served elaborate dinners with
red and white wines
There was champagne with dessert
strong coffee in a demitasse
and the ladies wore long dresses

When I entertain
I use oven-proof dishes
stainless-steel flatware
and serve a casserole, a salad
a glass of wine
and a nonfat dessert
There is decaf in a cup
and the women wear pants

When our daughters entertain
they use paper plates
order a pizza with beer
and get a store-bought cake
There is instant coffee in a mug
and everyone comes in jeans

When our granddaughters entertain
it will be pot luck
fast food in cardboard boxes
with soft drinks and coffee in paper cups
and everyone will sit on the floor
in sweat pants and T-shirts

So now I wonder what the generations
after that will do

To Grandmother's House for the Holidays

The tree is up and decorated
the presents are wrapped
the table is set with the best tablecloth
good china and crystal
the silver is shined

The aunt from Orange County
is making her *famous* pumpkin pie
The cousin from L.A.
his *famous* salad
The uncle is bringing
his *famous* cranberry relish
and the niece, her *famous* sweet potatoes
The children are bringing
only their *famous* children

While I have in the oven
a not-so-famous turkey
with non-famous stuffing
and boring, but good-for-you, vegetables

The guests are cheerful and noisy
the children at the children's table
have only one fight and no one cries

We eat a lot and drink a lot
and raise our cholesterol levels
The children get apple juice
and clamor for pizza
which, being a good grandmother
I have in the freezer

We talk and laugh and gossip
about those not there
They all leave with leftovers
in empty cottage-cheese containers
saved for the occasion
with sleepy children in their arms
and then I'm left with
three loads for the dishwasher
a tablecloth with gravy spots
and candle drippings
ribbons and torn wrappers
some of which I fold and put away for next year
half-eaten candy in an ashtray
jam on a chair
one shoe under the sofa
something spilled on the rug
a traumatized dog
and one exhausted grandmother

Authority Figures?

I weigh a few pounds too many
according to the clothes designers
who want all women to look like
anorexic twenty-year-olds

I don't look young enough
according to the advertisers
who sell hair dyes
and anti-wrinkle creams

I'm wearing the wrong clothes
according to the magazines
who dictate the length of our skirts
and the colors of our wardrobes

In a nation of conformists
do we dare to stand out
by looking our age
with a few extra pounds
wearing last year's clothes?

What Do I Really Want?

I want to write a book
but don't like the writing

I want to eat gourmet food
but don't like the cooking

I want to be slim
but don't like to diet

I want to be athletic
but don't like to exercise

I want to wake up early
but don't like getting up

I want nice clothes
but don't like the price tags

I want high-tech equipment
but don't like reading the instructions

I want good friends
but don't have enough time for them

I want it all
but don't like the effort

The Grass Is Always Greener

When I'm hot in the summer
I dream of winter's snow
When I'm cold in the winter
I long for summer's warmth

When I was a child
I wanted to be grown up
When I was twenty
I wished to be older
When I was middle-aged
I wanted to be twenty
When I reached retirement
I wished to be middle-aged

And so I went through life
never having what I wanted
instead of delighting in what I had

And now that I'm much older
I have learned to savor
each moment
and have no regrets
over what might have been

Little Pleasures

I will never win the Nobel Prize or the Pulitzer
I will never get an Oscar or an Emmy
I will never be on the cover
of *Time* magazine
or cited for anything world shaking

So I will have to make do
with getting excited
about finding a parking space
getting served quickly in a restaurant
not standing in line at the movies
I will find pleasure
in a walk with my dog
the sound of birds in the morning
a bowl of hot soup by the fireplace
a glass of iced tea on a summer day
I will appreciate
a kiss
a smile
a good joke
a phone call from a friend
my kids remembering my birthday

Come to think of it
I don't need a Pulitzer or an Oscar
for I have an award far greater than these...
the sweet names of family and friends
to call on at any time

About the Author

Natasha Josefowitz calls herself a late bloomer, having earned her master's degree at age forty and her Ph.D. at age fifty. She is an adjunct professor at the School of Social Work at San Diego State University, a noted columnist, and the author of three books on management, a book for children, a book for couples, and eight books of humorous verse, including her recent bestseller, **Too Wise to Want to Be Young Again**.

Dr. Josefowitz is an internationally known speaker, having lived and worked abroad and in the U.S. Her efforts on behalf of women have earned her numerous awards, including **The Living Legacy Award** from the Women's International Center and **The Women Helping Women Award** from the Soroptimist International. She has been named **Woman of the Year** five times by various national and international organizations, including the Women's Management Association, and was also honored by California Women in Government for her contributions to education.

Natasha is the mother and stepmother of five children and has seven grandchildren and step-grandchildren. She is grey-haired, wrinkled, and has a few extra pounds, but says she can celebrate life because she has PMZ (Post-Menopausal Zest).

Traveling in My Kitchen

French fries
English muffins
Danish pastry
Turkish delights
Russian borscht
Greek salad
Italian sausage
Swiss cheese
Belgian endive
German kraut
Chinese cabbage
Mideastern pita bread
Nova Scotia salmon
New York cheesecake
Boston lettuce

Dutch treat